Dear Parent:
Your child's love of readi...

Every child learns to read in a different way and at his or her own speed. Some go back and forth between reading levels and read favorite books again and again. Others read through each level in order. You can help your young reader improve and become more confident by encouraging his or her own interests and abilities. From books your child reads with you to the first books he or she reads alone, there are I Can Read Books for every stage of reading:

SHARED READING
Basic language, word repetition, and whimsical illustrations, ideal for sharing with your emergent reader

BEGINNING READING
Short sentences, familiar words, and simple concepts for children eager to read on their own

READING WITH HELP
Engaging stories, longer sentences, and language play for developing readers

READING ALONE
Complex plots, challenging vocabulary, and high-interest topics for the independent reader

ADVANCED READING
Short paragraphs, chapters, and exciting themes for the perfect bridge to chapter books

I Can Read Books have introduced children to the joy of reading since 1957. Featuring award-winning authors and illustrators and a fabulous cast of beloved characters, I Can Read Books set the standard for beginning readers.

A lifetime of discovery begins with the magical words **"I Can Read!"**

Visit www.icanread.com for information
on enriching your child's reading experience.

To parents who will be reading
this book to your children—
RAP IT!

I'm Rappy the Raptor
and I'd like to say,
I may not talk
in the usual way.
I'm rapping at the seashore.
I'm rapping in the snow.
I'm always rapping
wherever I go.

RAPPY

Goes to Mars

To Tamar —D.G.

To Charlie Huff, my son-in-law in

the "Rocket City" —T.B.

I Can Read Book® is a trademark of HarperCollins Publishers.

Rappy Goes to Mars
Text copyright © 2017 by Dan Gutman
Illustrations copyright © 2017 by Tim Bowers
All rights reserved. Manufactured in China.
No part of this book may be used or reproduced in any manner whatsoever without written permission except
in the case of brief quotations embodied in critical articles and reviews. For information address HarperCollins
Children's Books, a division of HarperCollins Publishers, 195 Broadway, New York, NY 10007.
www.icanread.com

ISBN 978-0-06-225268-5 (pbk.)
ISBN 978-0-06-225269-2 (hardcover)

17 18 19 20 21 SCP 10 9 8 7 6 5 4 3 2 1   ❖   First Edition

I Can Read!

READING 2 WITH HELP

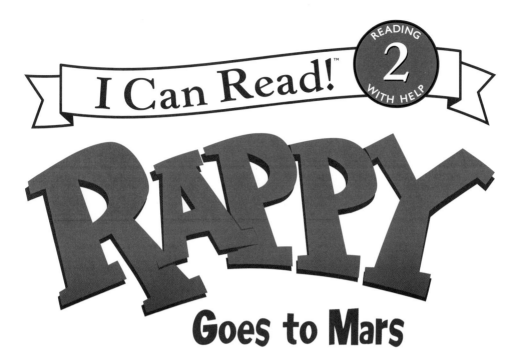

RAPPY
Goes to Mars

by Dan Gutman
illustrated by Tim Bowers

HARPER

An Imprint of HarperCollinsPublishers

It was recess.

I was lying on the grass.

Then I was flying

on the monkey bars

and crying, "This is fun!"

to cousin Simon.

Simon was climbing.

I was rhyming.

Suddenly, with perfect timing,

I looked up high.

I don't know why.

In the blink of an eye

THERE WAS SOMETHING

IN THE SKY!

The thing I saw was round and yellow.

"What is it?" somebody bellowed.

It had a shiny metal coating.

You could see that it was floating.

I heard a strange and awful noise.

All the girls and all the boys

forgot about our math and spelling.

We were shouting.

We were yelling.

The thing gave off a creepy glow.

I knew it was a UFO!

Cousin Simon ran for cover
as the flying saucer hovered.
Other kids began to scatter
but to me it didn't matter.
I couldn't move.

I was frozen.

It was like I had been chosen.

"Help me—I'm so scared!" I said.

It was right above my head!

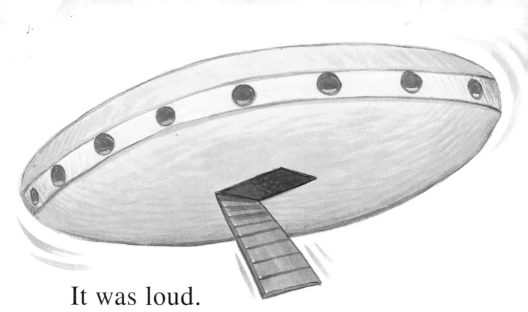

It was loud.

It was buzzin'.

I shouted out to find my cousin.

Then a door began to open.

Simon hollered, "Throw a rope in!"

It seemed like I was in a dream.

I saw a purple tractor beam.

The colored light surrounded me.

That UFO astounded me.

I just couldn't believe my eyes

when my feet began to rise!

The ship was filled
with seven crewmen.

None of them looked close to human.

They were thin and kind of hairy.

It was just a little scary.

And they had enormous eyes
about the size of apple pies.

Suddenly there was a rumble.

I lost my balance, took a tumble.

I crawled halfway 'cross the floor

trying to get to the door.

I thought that

I might be the last off.

Then the ship began to blast off!

I said good-bye to my home planet.

An alien (her name was Janet)

told me I should hold my ears.

"It's time to leave the atmosphere.

Don't try yelling.

Don't try clapping.

In space no one can

hear you rapping."

The UFO was shaking me.

I asked, "Where are you taking me?"

But Janet didn't scream or shout.

She just whispered, "You'll find out."

It was the most amazing trip.

Janet drove and steered the ship.

She was careful to avoid

the meteors and asteroids.

There were lots of knobs and dials.

We must have gone a zillion miles.

I was looking at the stars

when we landed right on Mars!

19

It looked like she was
going to strike me,
but Janet told me that she liked me!

She said that I was kind of cute.

I really didn't give a hoot.

What happened next was quite bizarre:

Janet said, "You're king of Mars!"

Then I was picked up and carried.

Janet said, "We're getting married!"

"But I'm too young to be wed!"

"I'm your wife now," Janet said.

What was I supposed to do?

I didn't have a single clue.

I don't want to be a ruler.

Going home would be much cooler.

This was worse than diarrhea!

But then I got a great idea!

"I'm Rappy the Raptor,"

I started to say,

"and I can rap the Milky Way.

I'm rappin' on Mars.

I'm rappin' on a comet.

I'll rap up in the stars

until you want to vomit."

"I rap in a pattern
and I'm such a genius.
I'll do a rap on Saturn,
or maybe even Venus.

Rapping is fun.

I'll rap on Jupiter.

Or maybe on the sun.

But that would be stupider.

I'll rap on all the planets,

and just in case I missed 'em.

I promise you, Janet,

I'll rap the solar system."

Janet was twitching.

She was jerking.

I could see my rap was working.

She was starting to turn red.

Then she looked at me and said,

"No more rapping!

I can't stand it!

Keep him quiet!

I demand it!

Let's send back this dinosaur.

I can't take it anymore!"

My teacher wasn't very happy.

She looked mad

when she yelled, "Rappy!

Recess ended hours ago.

What took you so long?

Why so slow?"

I didn't want to tell her

that I had an interstellar

trip across the universe.

That would only make things worse.

Rapping in space was really cool,

but from now on, I'll rap in school!